MW00387188

SERIES

Vol. 4

Shut the GATES

Purity in the Bedroom

Dr. June Dawn Knight

TreeHouse Publishers
Dreams Come True in Our House!

Copyright © 2017 Dr. June Dawn Knight

TreeHouse Publishers

www.gotreehouse.org

All rights reserved.

ISBN-13: 978-1541343610

ISBN-10: 1541343611

DEDICATION

This book is dedicated to my mother who passed away at the end of writing this book. Wilma JJ Bracey from Nashville, Tennessee. She found the Lord after she saw how He changed my life back in 1989. She gave her life to Him and never looked back. She was a loving mother and grandmother. She mothered children who were abandoned and alone. She fed the homeless and took them in too. She had such a big heart and is now in Heaven with her mother. I love you Mom and miss you greatly! I will see you soon!

Wilma "JJ" Bracey – 2/17/1941 to 01/22/2017

CONTENTS

Acknowledgments   i

Introduction   ii

1   Your Identity   Pg 1

2   Guard the Gates   Pg 5

3   Purity in the Bride   Pg 23

4   Purity in the Bedroom   Pg 33

5   Examples of Sexual Sin & Consequences   Pg 59

6   How to Shut the Gates   Pg 75

7   Prayer for Deliverance & Freedom   Pg 83

About the Author   Pg 85

ACKNOWLEDGMENTS

I want to acknowledge my children who have seen their mother follow in the fleshly footsteps and the sin that resulted. I am so thankful for their love and forgiveness. Now I can help others to not go down that road and to follow after holiness and righteousness. My children see a mother now that is protecting the anointing and walking with Jesus as her husband. I pray they are happy with the person that God has made their mother to be. I couldn't be this woman without the Lord! I give Him ALL the glory and praise!

INTRODUCTION

This book is number four in the *We are the Bride Series*. This series is dedicated to purity issues pertaining to the Bride of Christ. In previous books we touched on walking organically before the Lord and natural in relationship with our Creator. We discussed dropping all pretenses, religion, past beliefs, etc., and throwing our hands up to Heaven in a reckless abandonment to discover Him in a very real way. God has presented my life as an example to the struggles we humans face when battling whether to be obedient to God or just surrender all. I have been very transparent in my past frailties and errors in hopes that it will set others free. I am of no reputation and I am only writing these books in obedience to my first love.

God wants the Bride to experience His love and relationship that is unique to each person. I pray that this series has helped you to examine the way you see God and how religion has played such a vital part in your understanding of who He is.

This book will tackle a very sensitive subject in the Body of Christ, which is sex. Why talk about it? Because God is calling His Bride to be pure and holy and ready for His coming. He wants the lamps cleaned and polished for the Groom to arrive for His Bride. We must expose the enemy and the lies he presents to the church to cause them to be tainted and separated from the fullness of God. This book will confront various issues pertaining to sex and purity.

If you have read my other books, you know that I have been transparent with my life, the shortcomings I've experienced in my past, and my struggles; as well as the battle to accept my calling and destiny. I am writing a book about purity as the ex-woman-at-the-well!

Yes, I've been married several times and had a sex addiction in my past. I've been single now for 16 years. I'm not the expert on sex, but I have a grasp on understanding both sides of the coin. The worldly side that says "just do it" and the godly side that says, "die to yourself and remain pure."

I've remained pure and holy; chaste for years now with the understanding that Jesus is my true husband and I'm owned by Him and whoever wants to marry me this last time must go before God and receive permission to partner with God and marry this temple. Yes, the Lord has told me that I will marry again one day. Until that time comes, I remain separated for His will in my life.

My writing is presented through the perspective of a woman who has been there and done that. Since I've accepted His will for my life, I've had to fight the demons within myself and have them cast out, continually dying to my passions, and serve the Lord with all my heart. This life that I have chosen is where this book stems from and I pray that my mistakes will help you to be an overcomer and you will not go down the same road I did. If you read my testimony book, *Testimony of a Broken Bride; Jesus is the True Husband*, you will read of a woman who was molested and taken down a dark path in order to destroy her life destiny. Now that I've received healing and deliverance, God is using what the devil meant to destroy me with for His glory!

Topics Covered

Singles:

How are we to be pure as a single person? How can the gates get opened? What is permissible and what are my gates? Should I date around to see what I like? Is anything wrong with kissing and foreplay; as long as I'm not having sex with the person?

What about cybersex? If we're not actually physical, what's wrong with it? What is unequally yoked? How do I know who is the right one? How can I walk pure in this wicked world? What about being in leadership as a single person? Why am I treated differently than married leadership?

How can I stay pure until I get married or be united with Jesus at death? Is it OK to live with someone before marriage to test the waters in case it doesn't work out after marriage?

One out of two marriages end in divorce anyway; why get married?

Homosexuality:

What's the big deal with homosexuality? Who are you to tell me who I can love? I can't change my heart. I follow it and it tells me who to love. The world accepts it, why can't the church? Why is it unnatural? What does the Bible say about it? How is the Bible still relevant today when the whole world is accepting this practice? How can you say that demons are a part of this? This is not a choice, it is my heart and I'm born this way. What does purity have to do with my decision to love the same sex?

Marriage:

If I'm married, I'm already pure because I'm with one partner. Why do I need to worry about staying pure in the bedroom when the Bible clearly states;

> *Hebrews 13:4 - Marriage is honourable in all, and the bed undefiled: but whoremongers and adulterers God will judge.*

If my spouse and I are in agreement with our sexual preferences, then how can anyone say it's not pure or right? Is sex spiritual warfare? Is sex only meant for procreation? Is oral sex and anal sex accepted in a marriage to the Lord? Is sex a spiritual experience as well as physical? Does God care about my sex life as a married couple?

Virgins in Today's World:

Do virgins still exist? How can I stay a virgin with the whole world teaching opposite? Can I masturbate and do oral sex and still remain a virgin? Is it okay to have cybersex since no penetration? How can I stay a virgin? Is there a battle of the mind as a virgin Christian.

Sex with Demons or Spiritual World:

I'm not having sex with demons; I'm having sex with Jesus. It is passion and bridal love for my creator. How can this be demonic when it feels so real and is so passionate and erotic? The deception or misunderstanding of bridal intercession and bridal paradigm teaching and intimacy with God. The demons of Incubus and Succubus. What's wrong with having a spiritual wife or husband and having sex with it? At least I'm not at risk for a sexually transmitted disease, etc.

Sex with Animals – Bestiality:

Various countries make this practice legal so what's wrong with it? The dangers of this practice and the growing trend.

Transgender:

Who cares what God made me, I want to be the opposite. What if my natural habits lean towards habits and mannerisms of the opposite sex? What is wrong with changing genders? The world does it and accepts it; why can't the church?

Addictions, Perversions and Fetishes:

How can these things be dangerous to the Bride? What is it like to have an addiction to sex? What is perversion? In a marriage bed, sanctified by God, how can anything be perverted?

What are fetishes? What's wrong with having certain preferences towards sex? Can't I be unique in the bedroom?

Back to the Book:

This book will examine the various aspects of our sex life as Christians and how we can remain pure as the Bride of Christ. How can we be different in a world that is screaming so loud? How can we keep the gates shut and fulfill the destiny that God has for us? Can we really do this?

We will talk about how you have been bought with a price. Your body is not your own and God wants to use that temple for His glory. As His Bride, He wants you to be fulfilled and happy as a unique individual in every way!

Why should we shut the gates? How do we shut the gates? These answers will be presented in this book for you to consider and bring before God in prayer. I'm not saying my interpretation of the gospel is the perfect and right way for the Bride. I'm merely bringing another perspective and revelation for you to consider and bring before God in prayer and allow Him to reveal it to you. We are all held accountable to God for our own walks. Please just consider this perspective and see if God will help you to achieve your destiny in full as His Bride in preparation for His coming! Let's keep our lamps clean! No compromise! Shut the gates!

1
YOUR IDENTITY

The Bride of Christ is under severe attack from the enemy to dwindle the light and purity from the Earth. He's a roaring lion seeking whom he may devour. He is relentless and will not quit until you fold. The only way to resist him is with our decision to put our foot down and stand up for righteousness and obey the will of the one who sent us. Maintaining our prayer life and intimacy with God is the only way we can resist the devil and maintain this purity walk/holiness. Only through the Holy Spirit's help can we maintain walking in the spirit and resisting the temptations of the devil.

Unless the Bride knows her place in God, she cannot resist the devil and his scheming tactics. She must be fully assured of who she is and not budge off of that. In our prayer life and relationship with our Creator, we are able to maintain confidence in our position in Christ that will help us to overcome.

Knowing our identity is vital in order to protect what is on the inside of us. We must also lead a life of fasting so that we may continually die to our flesh. We must understand that we have been bought with a price and our bodies are no longer ours. Jesus bought it when He died on the cross. When He purchased our temple, we no longer have the authority to do anything with our temple that we want to. We are required to follow rules and regulations which are spelled out in the word of God.

These rules protect our temples and keep us clean before God. Without cleanliness (purity) we cannot see God. (Matt. 5). God is coming back after a church without spot or wrinkle (Eph. 5:27). This is purity.

An excerpt from my Organic Christianity Book

As I minister in various prisons, I realize one of the greatest attacks of Satan upon the Church today is in our identity. Satan tries to convince the Church that its members do not have self-worth and attempts to distract them from their destiny and calling.

If the Church does not have the revelation that they are the Bride of Christ with all rights to the inheritance that God has provided for them, they will not achieve the destiny that God designed for them before time began. Over 51% of the prisoners in the United States are incarcerated due to drugs. Less than one percent is due to murder. The rest are due to identity crisis sins such as robbery, etc. These statistics are from prison training I've had in various prisons. I'm sure it's as shocking to you as it was for me.

I pray this book will open your eyes to God's true calling and purpose for your LIFE.

God specifically designed each human for a reason. The reason is to give humans a choice as to whether or not he will serve God. If a person CHOOSES to allow God to finish their LIFE destiny book, then they will reveal another aspect of who God is to humanity. We are all here to provide a revelation of who God is. One human may reveal how great His mercies are for mankind. Another may reveal how He is a healing God.

Another person may reveal how, if humanity trusts God, He will be the true husband and provider, etc. Each human has a divine reason for being on Earth.

When a person makes the choice to surrender his life to his Creator, they realize that God can take anyone's nothingness and make them into something.

We are on Earth in God's Great Garden. This book delves into this beautiful place for us to respect and enjoy.

Like a tree in God's Great Garden, we are commanded to bear good fruit. If a tree bears good fruit, it is alive and well-nourished on the inside. If a tree does not bear fruit, it is withered and dry on the inside. We want to bear much fruit for the Kingdom of God.

My Identity Crisis and Sexual Gate

In my second book, *Testimony of a Broken Bride: Jesus is the True Husband*, I talk about the struggle of the call on my life.

I found the Lord as a little girl and developed a relationship with him in the woods. He was my peace in the midst of the storm. The book explains how sex was perverted to me since I was five years old. A loss of innocence and the twisting of Satan to the purity of sex resulted in a woman doing desperate things to survive. I was a sex addict and very bitter towards men because of the years of abuse, sexual deviancy, etc.

I had a twisted view of sex! At least I was getting something in exchange for what I was freely giving away. I know it sounds goofy, but at that time, it was my motive. So, for God to turn someone like that around and cause her to see the purity and holiness of God…WOW. What a God?

He can take someone like that and cause her to write books on purity and to tell and warn other people to SHUT THAT GATE. I now know that it is a device of the enemy to destroy your destiny and calling. It's an open gate that God wants SHUT so that He can bless you.

2
GUARD THE GATES TO THE GARDEN

In *Organic Christianity* book, I reveal that the Garden represents our prayer time with the Lord. I talk about us not allowing anything to interfere with our time in the Garden and the fellowship with our Creator. Our Garden is inside us as we are the temple of the Holy Spirit. We house God within our weak bodies. We can have a conversation with the Holy Spirit (God) no matter what is going on in the outer circumstances of our world.

We can either pray out loud, softly, or inwardly. We can talk to God through our hearts. This is why He is the judge of man's heart because the Bible says, "Out of the heart the mouth speaks." (Matt. 15:18). If World War III were happening right now and bombs were flying all around us, we can still pray. If they duct-tape our mouths and tie us up to cut our heads off, we can still talk to God. Our Garden is accessible 100% of the time and it has gates around it.

There are many teachings out there about gates; however, the gates I present in this book are from my revelation from God. Please pray and ask Him to reveal this to you. I present that there are many gates into our garden.

5

Examining the Gates

In my book, *Organic Christianity; Back to the Garden*, I reflect about the gates that we can open to our tree (I compare us to trees). My whole book, *Organic Christianity*, is dedicated to our identity.

So far we have discussed the five-fold senses and how it imparts seeds.

The Vision (eyes)
The Hearing (ears)
The Touching (hands)
The Tasting (mouth)
The Smelling (nose)

Due to the revelation about the seeds, we must block seeds from entering our tree by protecting the garden and gates. You know the old saying, "What comes in will come out." Now that we discussed the way we can pass seeds from tree to tree or from environment to our trees, we must protect the gates into our tree:

Eye Gate
Ear Gate
Mouth Gate
Hand Gate
Sexual Gate
Heart Gate

Each one of these gates will allow things in and if we're not careful it will express itself through an exit out of the tree, or an action of sin/disobedience to God.

Sexual Gate

I'm going to start with the sexual gate because the spirit of antichrist is deceiving so many people in this area. I can testify to this as I was deceived greatly in this area.

We all know that the Bible describes marriage as the institution between man and woman. God created sex for this institution.

> *Genesis 1:28-29 - God created man in His image; in the Divine image he created him; male and female He created them. God blessed them, saying: "Be fertile and multiply; fill the earth and subdue it."*

It is something to be enjoyed in the right environment. For instance, the Bible says that the marriage bed is undefiled.

> *Hebrews 13:4 - Marriage is honorable in all, and the bed undefiled: but whoremongers and adulterers God will judge.*

This means that God meant for husband and wife to enjoy the marriage bed. Satan destroys this image of perfect unity between a man and woman and attempts to defile the perfect union.

The ultimate defilement is homosexuality. The reason it is so impure is because it goes against nature itself. This means it goes against the whole purpose of God creating mankind.

According to this scripture reference, the ones who open themselves up to homosexuality also open themselves up to a whole pack of demons. Check this out on what attaches itself to this seed:

7

Romans 1:26-32 [26] For this cause God gave them up unto vile affections: for even their women did change the natural use into that which is against nature: [27] And likewise also the men, leaving the natural use of the woman, burned in their lust one toward another; men with men working that which is unseemly, and receiving in themselves that recompense of their error which was meet.

[28] And even as they did not like to retain God in their knowledge, God gave them over to a reprobate mind, to do those things which are not convenient;

[29] Being filled with all unrighteousness, fornication, wickedness, covetousness, maliciousness; full of envy, murder, debate, deceit, malignity; whisperers, [30] Backbiters, haters of God, despiteful, proud, boasters, inventors of evil things, disobedient to parents, [31] Without understanding, covenant breakers, without natural affection, implacable, unmerciful: [32] Who knowing the judgment of God, that they which commit such things are worthy of death, not only do the same, but have pleasure in them that do them.

The Bible talks about the impact of having sex outside of the marriage confines within God's blessing:

1 Corinthians 6 15-20 [15] Know ye not that your bodies are the members of Christ? Shall I then take the members of Christ, and make them the members of an harlot? God forbid. [16] What? know ye not that he which is joined to an harlot is one body? for two, saith he, shall be one flesh. [17] But he that is joined unto the Lord is one spirit. [18] Flee fornication. Every sin that a man doeth is without *the body; but he that committeth fornication sinneth against his own body. ¹⁹ What? know ye not that your body is the temple of the Holy Ghost which is in you, which ye have of God, and ye are not your own? ²⁰ For ye are bought with a price: therefore glorify God in your body, and in your spirit, which are God's.*

When you open your tree up to the sexual gate, you are opening it up to the other tree's demons and seeds. They enter your tree and take root. All the seeds I mention in this book, if we do not remove them from our tree, they will take root and sprout up at some time in our lives.

There are others who say that sex opens up the gate for soul ties. I'm not the expert in this subject, but I do know that I had them. I had to renounce my activities and break all ties with the soul-ties from previous attachments. Soul ties can be present without the prerequisite of sex. You can have a soul tie to a mean mother and it continually haunt you. You must then pray to release that soul tie that torments you.

I pray you understand a little about the Sexual Gate. God only created it to be within the confines of marriage. Thus, it should be guarded carefully and remain closed until the appropriate time.

This gate is so important because it can produce life or death. This is the gate where the seed is released from the man (husband) into the woman (wife) to impregnate her with life. This seed produces life and is holy before God. God then releases a spirit from Heaven to Earth. In the end, all spirits return to God.

> *Ecclesiastes 12:7 - Then shall the dust return to the earth as it was: and the spirit shall return unto God who gave it.*

It can bring death due to sexually transmitted diseases. If someone we partner with has an STD, then it could kill us. We must protect that gate and our temple.

The Bible also talks about the husband and wife becoming one when married. A marriage is consummated by sexual intercourse. Until they come together in this manner it is not even legal. What happens when they come together? In the perfect world when the groom enters the wife, it breaks her hymen and causes her to bleed. This is a prophetic significance of the covenant between man, wife and God. It's almost like an animal sacrifice. The humans broke the blood and gave the animal to the Lord. The blood ran down the alter. It's the same concept. When you think about it, a beautiful process takes place both physically and spiritually.

In another sense, both husband and wife are locked together and become one physically. It is a joining in the spirit as well as the flesh. What he has on the inside is joined into her and same with her. However, outside of the marriage covenant, this is dangerous.

It truly is a mystery. However mysterious, it is spiritual warfare.

The Mouth Gate

This is the hardest gate to keep closed. The Bible says it is an unruly member. It also says that we can speak life or death. I talk about this a lot when I discussed the audible seeds, but I do need to reflect on the gate of the mouth.

Proverbs 18:21 - Death and life are in the power of the tongue: and they that love it shall eat the fruit thereof.

I found this powerful teaching about words:

Our words carry power. They are spiritual seeds, which we "plant" to bring forth a harvest of one type or another. I'm not just talking about our words of prayer, but whatever words we use. Everything we do in the spirit realm is through our words. We pray with words, we worship with words, we break curses with words, we cast out demons with words, and we bless with words. Every word we speak enters the spirit realm and causes some effect. (Murphy, 2004)

Through this gate, if we're not careful, we can allow demonic activity to be released into our lives.

If we speak death and curses over ourselves, we grant the enemy permission to wreak havoc over our lives.

Example:

One day, Jesus and His disciples were walking from Bethany to Jerusalem. Jesus was hungry, and decided to eat. Unfortunately, the fig tree that He wanted to eat from didn't have any fruit on it, so He cursed it.

Mark 11:13-14 [13] *And seeing a fig tree afar off having leaves, he came, if haply he might find anything thereon: and when he came to it, he found nothing but leaves; for the time of figs was*

11

not yet. ¹⁴ And Jesus answered and said unto it, No man eat fruit of thee hereafter forever. And his disciples heard it.

Mark 11:20 - And in the morning, as they passed by, they saw the fig tree dried up from the roots.

What happened to the tree? The force of the curse that Jesus spoke forth took hold of that tree and killed it. Had He spoken a blessing over it, the tree would have been blessed. But, since He spoke a curse over it, it died. (Murphy, 2004)

As I said previously, what comes in will come out. What releases out of our mouth; we will answer on Judgment Day.

Matthew 12: 33-37 ³³ Either make the tree good, and his fruit good; or else make the tree corrupt, and his fruit corrupt: for the tree is known by his fruit. ³⁴ O generation of vipers, how can ye, being evil, speak good things? for out of the abundance of the heart the mouth speaketh.

³⁵ A good man out of the good treasure of the heart bringeth forth good things: and an evil man out of the evil treasure bringeth forth evil things. ³⁶ But I say unto you, That every idle word that men shall speak, they shall give account thereof in the day of judgment. ³⁷ For by thy words thou shalt be justified, and by thy words thou shalt be condemned.

This can be compared to the audible seeds as well. As far as being held accountable for what enters our body through the mouth gate, we are not warned against this:

> *Matthew 15:11 - Not that which goeth into the mouth defileth a man; but that which cometh out of the mouth, this defileth a man.*

Needless to say, our mouth can be a lethal weapon. It can slice and dice a human without any other weapon.

I would like to add one more way to use our mouth gate for God's glory, which is smiling. Did you know a smile can make someone's day? A smile can literally change the mood for someone who is depressed or hurting.

> *Proverbs 15:13, 30 [13] - A glad heart makes a happy face: a broken heart crushes the spirit. [30] – A friendly smile makes you happy and good news makes you feel strong.*

Please notice how the first scripture says the heart can change the face. Also on the second verse it says if we change the face it changes the heart. Interesting.

The Ear Gate

Like I said earlier about the music, it is basically what we are allowing into our tree through this gate.

Also, think about hearing bad news. Once we hear it, we must figure it out within ourselves what to do with that information. Sometimes we say, "I wish you wouldn't have told me. I wish I didn't know this or that." The reason we say that is because now it is a seed and we must decide what to do about that seed.

If we are not careful we will make the wrong decision.

When I was partying and listening to that Hip-Hop sexual music, I could listen to certain songs when I was "in the mood." I knew those songs could take me where I wanted to go. Now that I have surrendered my tree to the Creator, I reject those types of songs and fill my tree with holy and pure songs. I know what songs cause me to romance my husband (Jesus).

I know what songs will take me into the throne room of worship. Music is a power.

In addition to music and the outer influences, we must consider what we hear. There is a difference between listening and hearing.

I can listen to worldly music in a grocery store, but I may not be hearing it. I may tune it out amongst the other noise in the room. This is why the Bible says, "Let you hear what the spirit is saying to the churches." It says this because it wants you to really listen and pay attention to what God is saying. It means that we have our full focus and attention on those words that we are hearing.

We must tune-out the noise and distractions and hear the spirit of the Lord for our temples. He wants our full attention. We need to understand what the spirit is trying to relay to us.

Isn't it interesting that faith comes by hearing and hearing by the word of God. Look at this scripture:

Romans 10:17 – So then faith comes by hearing, and hearing by the word of God.

Faith comes by hearing means when we hear what God is saying through His word, not just listening to it.

In turn, we will receive His words and it will build our faith. This means that we are focused on what He is saying. We have understanding of it and we receive it.

Hearing by the word of God means that the word of God is going to speak to us. His word does not return void. His words are life.

Look at this:

> **Hebrews 4:12 – For the word of God is quick and powerful, and sharper than any two-edged sword, piercing even to dividing asunder of soul and spirit, and joints and marrow, and is a discerner of the thoughts and intents of the heart.**

So, when we are hearing the word of God, it is examining our heart, piercing our soul and cleaning our hearts. The Bible says that the Holy Spirit is the searcher of man's hearts. It also says that the word of God is a mirror where we must face our self. The word is like an X-ray machine.

The Eye Gate

The eye gate is a way for our souls to reach out to the outside world. We look at things and ponder on them. We see things and consider them. What we see can bring seeds in, and then we must decide whether to bury the seed, act on the seed, or discard the seed. We may ask God to forgive us for what we saw. We may decide to act upon what we saw.

We may decide to think about it later or dismiss it. However, what come in is buried in the tree somewhere.

15

Consider how they do with what we've seen in movies with mentally insane people sitting in a chair and images flashing into their eyes. These images are horror pictures, terrorizing images, etc. It can drive someone mad when they see such devastating images. It can also make a person tolerant of something because they have seen so much of the seed that it is planted in them and has built a root.

The Bible talks about the lust of the eyes causing us much grief:

> *1 John 2:15-17 [15] Love not the world, neither the things that are in the world. If any man love the world, the love of the Father is not in him. [16] For all that is in the world, the lust of the flesh, and the lust of the eyes, and the pride of life, is not of the Father, but is of the world. [17] And the world passeth away, and the lust thereof: but he that doeth the will of God abideth forever.*

I also consider Eve when she ate of the fruit. She saw that it was good and took it. She lusted after that fruit, thus she acted on it.

The Hand Gate

The hand gate is a powerful gate in that through the hands people are delivered, healed and set free. God commands us to lay hands on people. There must be a reason that it's through the hands. Look at this:

> *Mark 16:17-18 [17] And these signs will follow those who believe: In My name they will cast out demons; they will speak with new tongues; [18] they[a] will take up serpents;*

and if they drink anything deadly, it will by no means hurt them; they will lay hands on the sick, and they will recover."

There is an impartation that takes place through hands. I was asking God how this happens. He reminded me that He is the vine, and we are the branches. Our hands represent His branches reaching out to humanity.

The Bible also states to lay hands suddenly on no man. This can be interpreted many ways. One way meaning that what they have can come back to you and enter into you.

Another way means that we are to be slow to anger and withhold our hands in reaction to someone or a situation. The other way means we are to be very careful and treasure the anointing on the inside of us and do not be sudden or rash about releasing that to just anyone. Either way, be careful about laying your hands on someone.

Hands are also used in a weapon of war. Your hands are a battlefield in the spirit. We lift our hands to praise God.

Psalm 144:1 - Blessed be the Lord my strength which teacheth my hands to war, and my fingers to fight:

This can also mean in the spirit. Our hands waving in the air is like waving palm branches of worship and offering in the air. The Bible says that the trees of the field clap their hands. I believe that is us!

Heart Gate

The enemy tries to come in through our emotions. The Bible says the heart is deceitful, thus we cannot trust it. We must trust His word over our heart any day!

We will want to do something because we have the heart or compassion for someone or something, but if God didn't tell you to do it, etc., then it can be a way for the enemy to step in.

The enemy tries to come in through our emotions. The Bible says the heart is deceitful, thus we cannot trust it. We must trust His word over our hearts any day! We may want to do something because we have the heart or compassion for someone or something, but if God doesn't tell you to do it, etc., it can be a way for the enemy to step in.

The main way the enemy comes in through the heart to destroy us is offense. If we accept the offense and not bounce it right back by saying out of our mouth, "I forgive you," it buries itself within our hearts and forms a root of bitterness. When we have opened that door to offense, we've opened a big gaping wound in our heart through which other sins may enter. We must forgive quickly and not allow it to take root.

Your heart can deceive you into sin as well. I have been confronted by homosexuals who have said, "How can you tell me I can't love someone?" I say, "Well, then is it OK for me to LOVE my son, or LOVE my father or cousin?" Then they say, "No that is incest." Then, I reply, "Oh, now you're measuring love? Hmmm. How is that different than you loving the same sex? What if I love my dog or horse? What if I want to love it and marry it?

I have feelings, and I truly love my animals." See, the heart is deceitful. Also, the heart may tell us to do something sinful because it wants it. However, we must consider that the heart is reacting out of what we put in there.

> *Proverbs 21:2 – Every way of a man is right in his own eyes: but the Lord pondereth the hearts.*

So, what if I fell in love with a married man based off of my loneliness or based off the lust I've allowed in?

I'm opening the door to sin. I could say, "But I love him." The truth is, you can choose to leave that situation and not go down that road.

It is also true that what we allow to come in will come out when we are under pressure. Just pressure someone, and see what comes out. If he curses, it's because of what is in his heart. We also may witness anger rising up real quickly when he has unresolved bitterness. Look at this scripture:

> *Luke 6:45 A good man out of the good treasure of his heart bringeth forth that which is good; and an evil man out of the evil treasure of his heart bringeth forth that which is evil: for of the abundance of the heart his mouth speaketh.*

Please reflect as well on the dream I wrote about in the *Organic Christianity* book about the big fluffy pretty tree in the forest and the arrows of offense flying towards it. The tree saw the arrow coming and had to choose on whether to let that offense in the heart or to push it back and say, "I forgive."

The difference is his reaction to the arrows. We must guard our hearts to keep evil out, and walk in forgiveness.

Forgiveness of the Heart

I must write about forgiveness because of the troubling times the Bride is entering into. Please pay attention to the enemy's tactics.

I studied media during graduate school, and I know how the main-stream media is run by a certain few. Some would argue that the Illuminati are the ones who control the gates of what comes into the mainstream news, television shows, movies, music, etc.

If you want to know more, read my book, *The Mark of the Beast*. It is about my trip to London in December 2011 through January 2012.

I discovered that they are chipping people today in Europe and the United States.

One thing for sure is that the spirit of antichrist is ruling the Earth, and it wants to instill anger in our hearts. The media purposefully shows us images and video to spark the reactions that they desire.

They may want Christians to let down their guard or to act a certain way to prepare them for their global agenda to chip all humans with an RFID (radio frequency identification device) tag. Some may argue that is the mark of the beast. So, how will they brainwash society to take this chip? They will just continue to show us scary situations like ISIS killing Christians.

One of the purposes is to instill anger in our hearts toward others. Please bear with me a minute as I explain. If we watch this and allow it to take root in our hearts, when they come to our door to kill us or torture us, what will come out of our hearts? Of course, it will be anger. God does not want that to happen. He wants us to forgive and love. It's hard to love when we are full of bitterness. Those are seeds that Satan wants to put in your temple. Shut that door so the seed cannot enter.

When you see situations like that on television, say in your heart, "I forgive them Lord." People do not realize that unforgiveness roots can come through the visual even though it may not be directly addressing them. It is what you see through the eye gate. I'm also addressing this as a way to enter the heart gate as well. We want to be like Stephen in the Bible where we will be full of God's love towards that person or people. We must love them until the death.

I have some friends that travel to Egypt and they say Muslims are being converted through forgiveness!

Protect your heart and walk in forgiveness. Unforgiveness builds hard roots and will clog up your relationship with God. I believe this is what happened to the church through the last president's term. The textbooks in colleges were full of white guilt and Christian's fault of history and purposely set racially divisive techniques to bring a great divide between white and blacks in America. If the Christian was not careful, they fell for this trap and voted for Hillary...although she was against everything Christians stand for. This is how offense works. It will cause sickness and other things. It's not worth it. Forgive.

The Importance of Mentors & Inner-Circle

We need a great cloud of witnesses around us. We need mentors and people who will keep their spiritual eyes open over our souls. They are watchmen on the wall. The enemy can't get through the gates because you're surrounded by protection. Our problem becomes when we do not want to hear from the wise counsel or we manipulate the wise counsel to achieve our goals.

When we surrender ourselves to our inner circle, and are truthful with them, we are protected by other eyes to guard our souls from the foxes. Only pride will keep us from accepting wisdom, criticism, instruction and rebuke. When we get to that place, we're basically backslidden because pride has raised its ugly head. We must stay humble and transparent before others so that the foxes are exposed. If we go through that door with pride as the key, the enemy is just waiting on the other side to destroy. Keep the gates closed, Bride. Trust those you have entrusted with your life.

Examples of Ignoring the Inner Circle

I must write about the dangers of ignoring the warning signs from those closest around you. When your friends begin telling you what they see and you begin "rationalizing" your behavior, you know you're in sin. When they tell you that they have an uneasy feeling about what you are doing, etc., then our reaction should be to go to the throne room and pray about it. Maybe your friends see something you can't see. God may be using that person to reveal to you a fox in the camp.

Compromise will kill your gate. It is like a cankerous sore that keeps bleeding out and begins tainting your healthy flesh.

Don't compromise Bride. Trust the people that God has surrounded you with. Your final trust is in the Lord. When someone confronts you with something they see, don't just blow it off and get mad at them for "judging you"...go to God in prayer and ask Him. Say, "June says that she sees me with lust (or whatever it is)...and I don't see it Lord. Will you reveal this to me if this root is in my heart? Please show me the truth Lord." Then the person has been transparent with God and asked Him to reveal their possible-deceitful heart. The Bible says that the heart is deceitful. Meekness doesn't get offended...it prays and asks God to either confirm it or to cast it off them. As a Christian we are to love being rebuked, chastised and corrected by God. Sometimes we let things in and do not even realize it. He will have other people to confront you if you're not listening to Him. He's probably already dealt with you many times and your hearing and vision may be clouded due to sin. So, do like Moses did and go to the Father and ask Him if those people are telling the truth. (Numbers 16).

Ask the Holy Spirit to reveal your heart.

Dr. June Dawn Knight

3
PURITY OF THE BRIDE

What is Purity and Why Do I Need It?

Purity means that we separate ourselves from evil and treasure the gift that God has given us in our temples. Our temples are the body that God has given us to steward while we're on Earth. Our temple may be uglier than other temples, older, more wrinkles, may have missing limbs, etc. Our temple may be prettier than other temples. We may feel we can make our temples prettier by adorning it with gold and silver or painting it. However, the body that God gave us when we came to Earth is the one that He chose for us. Due to society's view of beauty, we may feel less-than and not as worthy as other temples.

No matter the visual appearance of the temple, we are held accountable to God on how we steward (take care of) that temple. We only have one time on Earth to make this mission right, so we must not take it for granted. It is so easy to procrastinate and think we have forever to live, so we never deal with issues and keep on letting time go by.

Holiness and Purity to God

God is calling His Church back to holiness, consecration and purity. Holiness meaning sanctification and set apart for His good will and service.

According to Merriam-Webster Dictionary, the definitions of sanctification, sanctify, holiness, and consecration are:

Definition of Sanctification:
1. An act of sanctifying
2.   a. the state of being sanctified
B. the state of growing in divine grace as a result of
    Christian commitment after baptism or conversion
    (Merriam-Webster)

Simple Definition of Sanctify:
1. to make (something) holy
2. to give official acceptance or approval to (something)

Full Definition of sanctify:
sanc·ti·fied   sanc·ti·fy·ing
1. to set apart to a sacred purpose or to religious use
    consecrate
2. to free from sin : purify
3.   a. to impart or impute sacredness, inviolability, or respect
              to
b. to give moral or social sanction to

4. to make productive of holiness or piety <observe the day of
    the sabbath, to sanctify it — Deuteronomy 5:12 (Douay
    Version)> (Merriam-Webster)

Definition of Holiness:
    1. the quality or state of being holy
    Holiness —used in the titles of high religious officials

Full Definition of holiness:
1. the quality or state of being holy —used as a title for various
    high religious dignitaries <His Holiness the Pope>
2. sanctification 2 (Merriam-Webster)

Definition of Consecrate:
    1.   dedicated to a sacred purpose (Merriam-Webster)
    2.

As these definitions explain, it is the act of us setting ourselves apart for His will for our lives. It is being sheep and allowing our Great Shepherd to guide us. Look at what the Bible says about holiness:

> *1 Peter 1:14-16* [14] *As obedient children, not fashioning yourselves according to the former lusts in your ignorance:* [15] *But as he which hath called you is holy, so be ye holy in all manner of conversation;* [16] *Because it is written, Be ye holy; for I am holy.*

> *1 John 3:6-10* [6] *Whosoever abideth in him sinneth not: whosoever sinneth hath not seen him, neither known him.* [7] *Little children, let no man deceive you: he that doeth righteousness is righteous, even as he is righteous.* [8] *He that committeth sin is of the devil; for the devil sinneth from the beginning. For this purpose the Son of God was manifested, that he might destroy the works of the devil.* [9] *Whosoever is born of God doth not commit sin; for his seed remaineth in him: and he cannot sin, because he is born of God.*

> [10] *In this the children of God are manifest, and the children of the devil: whosoever doeth not righteousness is not of God, neither he that loveth not his brother.*

> *2 Corinthians 7:1 - Having therefore these promises, dearly beloved, let us cleanse ourselves from all filthiness of the flesh and spirit, perfecting holiness in the fear of God.*

> *Hebrews 12:14 - Follow peace with all [men], and holiness, without which no man shall see the Lord:*

> *1 Peter 2:9 - But ye [are] a chosen generation, a royal priesthood, an holy nation, a peculiar*

people; that ye should shew forth the praises of him who hath called you out of darkness into his marvelous light:

1 Thessalonians 4:7 - For God hath not called us unto uncleanness, but unto holiness.

2 Timothy 2:21 - If a man therefore purge himself from these, he shall be a vessel unto honour, sanctified, and meet for the master's use, [and] prepared unto every good work.

Leviticus 20:26 - And ye shall be holy unto me: for I the LORD [am] holy, and have severed you from [other] people, that ye should be mine

Isaiah 35:8 - And an highway shall be there, and a way, and it shall be called The way of holiness; the unclean shall not pass over it; but it [shall be] for those: the wayfaring men, though fools, shall not err [therein]

1 Thessalonians 5:23 - And the very God of peace sanctify you wholly; and [I pray God] your whole spirit and soul and body be preserved blameless unto the coming of our Lord Jesus Christ.

The reason sanctification and purity is so important in the Bride at this hour is because she must be without spot and wrinkle for her King. She is chosen by God to be living on Earth for such a time as this.

She must separate herself from the world and consecrate herself. Through purity, the anointing flows to develop fruit for the Kingdom of God. Purity is the key to relationship with God. It guarantees open-access to a holy God.

He says in His word that He hears the prayers of the righteous. He also says the prayers of a righteous man availeth much.

Walking in purity is walking in relationship with God 24 hours a day. It's a life of prayer at all times. When you have a free-relationship with God you may talk to Him in the middle of the night, in the shower, etc.

It is walking in the revelation that He is with you at all times and you have His full attention through relationship. It's open-access in the Garden and fellowship with your Creator.

What is Purity?

Purity is walking in right-standing with God because you are dead to your flesh and walk in the spirit with God.

You have surrendered your body, members, heart, and soul to the purposes of God. You have the revelation that you are not your own and you do not possess the rights to your flesh to do what you want with it.

> *1 John 3:2-3 ² Beloved, now are we the sons of God, and it doth not yet appear what we shall be: but we know that, when he shall appear, we shall be like him; for we shall see him as he is. ³ And every man that hath this hope in him purifieth himself, even as he is pure.*
>
> *Psalm 119:9 Wherewithal shall a young man cleanse his way? by taking heed thereto according to thy word.*
>
> *Matthew 5:8 Blessed are the pure in heart: for they shall see God.*

Philippians 4:8   Finally, brethren, whatsoever things are true, whatsoever things are honest, whatsoever things are just, whatsoever things are pure, whatsoever things are lovely, whatsoever things are of good report; if there be any virtue, and if there be any praise, think on these things.

Purity Opens the Heavens

When the Bride walks in purity and keeps the gates shut, it allows the windows of Heaven to remain open in their lives. Obedience is the key to the wealth from Heaven. Wealth is more than just money and provision. It is wisdom, favor, impartation, revelation, grace, etc. The Bride protecting his/her vessel and cherishing the one who resides on the inside of them can only bring the promises of God to them. It is not that the relationship is based on works, but it is in honoring God.

I said this before in my previous books that when I had to face the Lord about my sexual promiscuity, it was an eye-opening experience. When I faced my frailty and sin before a Holy God, I could only weep.

When I was sinning and just giving my body away so freely, I had no respect for my heavenly father. I truly did not know who I was. I'm still in progress of learning who I am in Him. Now I have the revelation that no one has the right to touch me or have access to this body because it is not my own.

When I made the decision to die to my will and desires, I chose to give Him my life like He chose to give His life for me. It is a Romeo/Juliet story.

The Perfect Will Versus the Permissive Will

Your will has everything to do with purity. You can choose to sin or choose to stand up for righteousness. The devil wants you to drop your will and to allow him to enter. If we don't stand strong, we will fall for the tactics of the enemy.

There is a big difference between perfect will versus permissive will. The perfect will is saying, "June, I want you all to myself because I'm a jealous God!" The permissive will says I may turn around and do because I can't die to ALL that He's asking me to do. I will still go to church all the time, serve my pastor to the fullest, and do everything else that is good in the world EXCEPT the ONE thing that God is asking me to do! That is the permissive will.

Another example – God tells Joe Blow to start preaching. Well, since he doesn't want to pay the full price to do God's perfect will, he starts a charity to help homeless people so that he can keep up his lifestyle that he wants. People in the community are praising him because he's doing such a noble thing. However, underneath the good actions, he's really in disobedience to God. So, God may have to allow things to happen to him because he is not obeying God.

FYI – when something happens to you whether in sickness or some type of tragedy, the first thing you should do is examine your heart. Go to God and say, "Lord, is there something I've done to cause this to happen? Have I opened the door to the enemy somehow?" So, we should always examine our hearts and make sure the door is shut to the enemy in our lives!

Once you know you're in 100% obedience to God's will, then just hang on for the ride and trust God.

4
PURITY IN THE BEDROOM

In this chapter we will address the various areas and how it plays a role in purity before God. Sex was created by God to be enjoyed in a pure and holy marriage. Religion and wrong doctrine stepped in and caused sex to be boring and sometimes shameful. It has been told to Christians that sex is only for child-bearing and not to be enjoyed. I beg to differ. God is unique and created us to be unique. He wants His creation to enjoy sex and the intimacy of the marriage union. My minister friend, Sharon Carter from Hermitage Tennessee said, "Sex in a marriage is spiritual warfare because God made them one and the enemy wants to keep unity out of the marriage. When couples come together during sex it creates a unity, which is holy before God." I tend to agree in that when a couple is making love that God is not turning His head and saying, "Oh no, my creation is having sex, don't look." No, I believe God makes the perfect three-fold cord; which is not easily broken. God is with that couple and He means it to be enjoyed.

In the confines of marriage (of course), God created each person unique and may have different erogenous points that turn them on. God created them unique like that and there is nothing wrong with couples "exploring" to discover those points/turn-ons.

Whether you are single, married, consider yourself transgender, homosexual, a virgin, a practicing bestiality, or have sex with demons (spirits); we need to discuss them from Christian life.

Naturally the world sees the issues differently than Christians because we are guided by the Holy Bible.

We are ultimately guided by the conscience (Holy Spirit). He will let you know if something is out of bounds and not good for you. Ask yourself, "Is what I'm doing defiling my own conscience?" If you're feeling shame or guilt about something, then go to God and ask Him why.

The following discussions are meant to be another perspective to consider when walking out your destiny. The Holy Spirit is your guide and teacher. He guided me to write this book so I pray it helps you.

Marriage

We will start off with marriage. The Bible says that sex (yes, oral sex too…it is sex) is only permissible within the bounds of a holy marriage. How do we define marriage? It is performed before a holy God and recognized by the government legally through a marriage certificate. It can be performed in a courthouse, outside, in a church, etc.; as long as it is legal by the government. Some Christians will try to say they are legally married before God because they said their vows before God and no one else and that is what matters. However, it must be legal and recognized by the government in order for it to be holy before God.

This is mainly relevant in America because of our country's laws. This may be different according to other cultures and religious practices (within Christianity of course). In America, we must go through the process of obtaining a marriage license.

The next step is to have a legal representative perform the ceremony and sign off on the certificate. We then must present the paperwork back to the state. In American culture, we must have a marriage certificate in order to be recognized for benefits in marriage.

Now that we have established what marriage is defined as, let's talk about sex within that holy union.

Marriage is definitely between a man and woman only. It is unnatural to be any other way. When a man and woman marry, they become one before God's eyes. It's really a mystery as to how this happens. According to the word of God, they become one flesh.

> **Mark 10:8   And they twain shall be one flesh: so then they are no more twain, but one flesh.**

Issues in Marriage Context:

If I'm married, I'm already pure because I'm with one partner. Why do I need to worry about staying pure in the bedroom when the Bible clearly states, "The marriage bed is undefiled."?

The scripture you are referring to is Hebrews 13:4 that says, "Marriage is honourable in all, and the bed undefiled: but whoremongers and adulterers God will judge." (KJV)

There are many ways you can defile the bedroom. Let's talk about those defilements:

- **Anal Sex** – Although both may agree to this action, it is still unholy in all its ways because it is first unnatural.

God did not create the anus to receive other objects being inserted. It is meant to be an exit-only place. This is common sense. Yes, I have heard many say that there is an erogenous place within the anus that can cause a man to have an orgasm in a powerful way (which is why they are drawn to it), but I believe this is evil. In my *Clarion Call to Unity* book, I talk about how scientists have seen a correlation to goats. They have the same gland. Goats also represent evil in the scriptures. Goats represent stubborn people (sinners) and sheep represent Christians because they follow.

- o Also when I think about anal sex I think about the upside down cross. Satan does things backwards in the way that God does it. By having humans resort to this form of sexual pleasure, it is a smack in God's face from the way He created humans and sex.
- o Anal sex is unhealthy. Doctors have proven the unhealthy factors involved in this activity. It brings bacteria into the wrong cavities.
- o Anal sex is a huge gate that will be opened to other perversion and demons. It may open up to the man being more tolerant to experience a homosexual lifestyle because he's already entering one anus, so why would a man's anus be any different (if he's horny enough). Shut this gate!

If the world says this practice is "normal"…it does not mean that God say it is. The world is operating by the Spirit of Antichrist. It is the spirit of this world and not to be trusted.

Oral Sex – I know this topic will be taboo, but oral sex is perfectly natural in a marriage. Of course there are so many extenuating circumstances with different people so it all boils down to each couple. A woman may not be comfortable with it because she was molested in the past and is not healed. She may have pain during the sex, etc. I'm just presenting the point that it is okay to have fun with oral sex within the marriage bounds; if you choose to do so.

- o God gave a woman a clitoris for one purpose only. It is given by God for the women to experience ecstasy. It is for the purpose of enjoyment for the female. Some people in the church teach against oral sex and talk about how licking and touching is not natural; thus this practice is not right.

- o I disagree with this theology. When you are in love with someone, you want to touch them all over and kiss them all over. You want to enjoy an intimacy with them that involves every part of your being. The oneness between the two is meant to be erotic and fun. Why should a couple ignore the clitoris? God gave it to the woman and it provides extra lubrication and enjoyment for both involved. God gave that organ for a reason and I believe He means for that to enhance the sexual experience.

- o Did you know that many cultures that demoralize women by actually castrating women and cut the clitoris off? Yes. They do not want women to enjoy sex or to have an advantage over the men.

- See, the men's part (penis) has a dual-function, to include urination. Their part is not strictly for pleasure like the woman's part. This causes the cultures of men-dominance to want to remove that enjoyment from women. In American culture, we do not castrate women. I'm just trying to get the point out there that the clitoris is very natural and given by God and meant to be enjoyed.
- Only religion tries to stifle that in marriages. I pray that you go before God and ask Him if you doubt this. Why would God give you something so enjoyable and not be able to use it? Why would He give it to couples? He gives it to couples because He wants them to have fun. We will delve more into this.
- The whole point of love is to give. When you love someone you want to please them and help them enjoy themselves as well. Yes, the pleasure should not be one-sided because that is selfish and could be control and manipulation (which is a sin). If you have a spouse that loves to give and you will not allow that spouse to enjoy it, then pray about it and ask God to help you to overcome and please your spouse.
- These scriptures I believe describes Solomon and his Bride being erotic in the bedroom:

Song of Solomon 4:10-16 - ¹⁰ How fair is thy love, my sister, my spouse! how much better is thy love than wine!

*and the smell of thine ointments than all spices! ¹¹
Thy lips, O my spouse, drop as the honeycomb:
honey and milk are under thy tongue; and the
smell of thy garments is like the smell of Lebanon.
¹² A garden inclosed is my sister, my spouse; a
spring shut up, a fountain sealed. ¹³ Thy plants are
an orchard of pomegranates, with pleasant fruits;
camphire, with spikenard, ¹⁴ Spikenard and
saffron; calamus and cinnamon, with all trees of
frankincense; myrrh and aloes, with all the chief
spices: ¹⁵ A fountain of gardens, a well of living
waters, and streams from Lebanon. ¹⁶ Awake, O
north wind; and come, thou south; blow upon my
garden, that the spices thereof may flow out. Let
my beloved come into his garden, and eat his
pleasant fruits.*

- o I interpret this scripture as talking about them experiencing oral sex and mad-passionate love-making. I know some people suggest it means Jesus and the Bride, but I see it as an example of how God created sex to be enjoyed.
- **Toys** – Some people say it's okay to play with toys as a married couple. There are several factors to consider when choosing this path. Number one – Do you not feel that if you bring a dildo in the bed with you that your wife is cheating on you? I can hear some say that the husband may be impotent and may have to do it to please his wife. This is a conviction that must be held between the couple. Just know that when you open the door to toys in your marriage that it may open other doors. I submit that this is unnatural because God did not create it so shut the gate!

- **Pornography or sexual videos** – This is most definitely a no-no. It is sexual perversion in all its ways. When you open your eye and ear gate to participate in fornication acts on your television, then you have participated in their sin and received it in your heart.
  - o This will open a wide gate in your marriage. The wife may grow unsatisfied because he does not do it like they do on the video or vice versa. It is also unrealistic. Most of the things you see on the videos are fake. The moaning, screaming, etc., it's all for show.
  - o I've prayed with many women who feel so distant from their husbands because he wants her to do the things he sees on the video. It demoralizes the women in so many ways. It's a huge tactic of the enemy to instill evil seeds in the one who watches it.

  So, shut this gate!

- **Masturbation in Marriage** – What is wrong if one spouse masturbates and the other does not? Here are factors you must consider about masturbation.

  - o If you both are in agreement and both involved, then that may be okay. However, there are a few things to consider:
  - o The problem comes in when the spouse does it behind the other one's back and may end up obsessed or it may dwindle the experience between husband and wife. So, why do it? In other words…they don't need you now.

o I met a woman one time that they were both ministers. She was heart-broken because he masturbated all the time and made her feel like she wasn't good enough to satisfy him and he couldn't get enough. At first I couldn't understand why that bothered her until the Lord convicted me over it. It is like he is cheating on her with his own self. Not only is he being a self-pleaser, but he is neglecting the needs of his wife. This is a sin within itself. Be careful with this gate!

o Another factor to consider is jealousy. If you are always pleasing yourself, then the spouse may feel that your arousal is more important to you than seeking the arousal through her. I know there are extenuating circumstances; which is great when both can come in agreement about their situation. I'm just giving you things to consider.

Shut this gate!

- **Swingers or Sharing/Bringing Others in the Bed** – This practice is growing like crazy! You would be surprised how many couples do this. There are swingers clubs everywhere.

  o The world attempts to make this seem acceptable but the Bible is strict about this subject.

  o This is adultery and we as Christians cannot participate in this action. Do I even need to address this further as to the dangers of this practice? This is a huge gate to shut!

- **Whips & Chains – Dominance & Submission in the Bedroom** – This is bigger than you know as well. This is definitely a huge no-no to Christians as well. Even if both of you agree to this action, it goes against nature. When considering your sexual acts; think on whether it is natural to do this or that. Did God create it? Did He mean this to happen? God does not mean for either party to be demoralized. I hear some of you say, "Yeah, but what if one person likes to be treated like that?" The answer is still no. You are sowing seeds into that person's spirit of anger, perversion, etc. Shut this gate!

Bride, I submit to you that in the confines of marriage covenant with a holy God, that He wants you to enjoy your sexual experience with your spouse. Have fun and ask God how you can please your spouse and cause them to have the ultimate enjoyment and experience with you. I think of that book *The Five Love Languages*. Each of us is different and will experience our sex time with our spouse different than other couples. As long as we are being natural and can do it with a clean conscience before God, then enjoy yourselves!

I merely wanted to show you other avenues that the enemy will try to creep in so that you can be aware and pray about shutting that gate. Unnatural ways such as anal sex, pornography, whips, chains, bringing others in, etc., is obvious. God does care about your sex life so talk to Him about it.

Being Single

As a single person, we are really not single. We are in a covenant relationship with Jesus. He is our husband (we are betrothed) and He owns us. So, basically when someone asks if you're married...we may say "Yes." How are we to be pure as a single person? How can the gates get opened in my life? What is permissible and what are my gates? Let's address a few issues:

- **Should I date around to see what I like?**
    - There is nothing wrong with dating as a whole, once you think you have found the right person. Why should you date someone you would not consider marrying? Are you not just wasting time and possibly opening the door for the devil to move in? The reason I say this is because you may open the door to kiss or be affectionate with other people. This type of affections should be preserved for the one that God has for you. Also, when you go on a date, you are surrendering your time and body to a person. You are giving them devoted time and the appearance to other people that they are a possible suitor. Here are considerations –
    - What will others think when they see you out with this person or various people all the time?
    - What if this person expects something in return because they either paid for your meal or gave you their time for the night?
    - It could be a distraction from your mission that God has called you to complete.

- **Is anything wrong with kissing and foreplay; as long as I'm not having sex with the person?**
    - When you asked Jesus into your heart, you chose to surrender your fleshly will to His will. You may not have known in full context what you did, but you decided to live according to the word of God and not your own.
    - Jesus bought your body with a price. He owns it. We no longer have the right to freely kiss and give affections to another outside the marital bounds. They must do it right according to the word of God and that is through marriage. When they want to marry you as the male, they must go to God in prayer and ask for your hand in marriage. Once God grants the request, then follow his leading on how to ask the woman and her father, etc.
    - So yes, all foreplay is wrong. Ask God to take away the desire until it can be fulfilled in marriage. God has designed us to have a sexual desire, but it is to be released with those confines. Shut the gate!

- **What about cybersex? If we're not actually physical, what's wrong with it?**
    - Cybersex or phone sex is wrong because you are submitting your imagination over to evil thoughts of lust and perversion. The Bible says to cast down every imagination that exalts itself against God. This is that case. Shut that gate!

- **What is unequally yoked? How do I know who is the right one?**
  - Mission is the most important reason as to why we should marry someone. Some people think it's whether they are a Christian or not, but I submit to you that it is mission.
  - What if God has called you to change the world and do this or that and you marry someone with no ambition or purpose? What if you marry someone who is called to be a pastor to one local church and you are called to be a missionary? What if you are an evangelist and your pastor spouse wants to be home all the time and does not approve of you being on the road?
  - I asked a minister one time, "How do we know if they are the right person or not?" He replied, "You will know when everyone around you in your circle is blessed by the union. When there is friction or doubts in others, then it's a huge red flag." I've always remembered this and I've seen it to be true over the years.
  - I've seen people date others and you can totally see the light dwindle from their eyes and others around them try to warn them and they rationalize themselves right into their sin. They continue and the enemy ends up taking them out or deceiving them greatly. They pay the price for their sin. Also, the Bible says that we are only tempted by the sin that is within our hearts.

- So, if a person is headed off in a sin of some sort, it is because they already had the sin in their heart before they acted on it.

- **How can I walk pure in this wicked world?**
  - You can remain pure as a single by seeking ye first the Kingdom of God and all the other things will be added unto you. Die to yourself and trust in God to bring you the right mate.

- **What about being in leadership as a single person?**
  - This dynamic situation is a whole added variable. When we are leadership in the Body of Christ, we are held to a higher standard. We are no longer babes in Christ, but sons of God. We are to walk in a spirit of excellence before God and man and be careful to carry our lives with dignity and honor before all men. Why? Because you are an ambassador of Christ. You represent the King of Kings and you are a walking Bible. People watch you. The Bible charges us not to be stumbling blocks to other people.

- **Why am I treated differently than married leadership?**
  - I have heard this from many single spiritual leaders. Married leaders seem to be treated with more respect. I don't know why; but Paul says in the Bible that it is better that we remain single and devoted to God and service to His kingdom.

- **Is it OK to live with someone before marriage to test the waters in case it doesn't work out after marriage? One out of two marriages end in divorce.**
  - This is a sin to live outside the bounds of marriage. The Bible does not support this action at all. Not only does the Bible say to refrain from all appearance of evil, but it also says fornicators go to Hell. I've heard some say that they do not sleep together in the same house. This does not matter because of the appearance of it. Not only are they living in sin, but they are giving the impression to the community that they do not trust God to provide for that home without the help of another. God is our provider and will take care of His people, if they will only trust Him. When we honor God by living Holy,

---

The Following Scriptures and commentary are from Ray Fowler at http://www.rayfowler.org/2008/05/21/scriptures-on-living-together-before-marriage/. Please check out this website for further information. It's very informative.

  - **Proverbs 14:12** – "There is a way that seems right to a man, but in the end it leads to death." This Scripture stands against the arguments, "Everyone is doing it. It's the new way. It's accepted in society." That may all be true, but just because a path seems right doesn't make it so.
  - **Ecclesiastes 3:1, 5** – "There is a time for everything and a season for every activity under

heaven ... a time to embrace and a time to refrain." As the following Scriptures indicate, the right time for living together is after marriage — not the year before, not the month before, not the night before. There is a time to embrace, and a time to refrain.

- **1 Corinthians 6:18** – "Flee from sexual immorality. All other sins a man commits are outside his body, but he who sins sexually sins against his own body." Living together almost always involves premarital sex. By living together before marriage, you dishonor both yourself and your partner.

- **1 Corinthians 7:8-9** – "Now to the unmarried and the widows I say: It is good for them to stay unmarried, as I am. But if they cannot control themselves, they should marry, for it is better to marry than to burn with passion." This isn't the place to get into why Paul recommends singleness over marriage in this particular passage. However, it is important to note that the Bible encourages a couple that is struggling with sexual temptation to marry rather than burn with passion. Of course, this assumes a couple that is ready for marriage. I recommend that all couples get good premarital counseling from a pastor or Christian counselor before getting married.

- **Galatians 6:7-8** – "Do not be deceived: God cannot be mocked. A man reaps what he sows. The one who sows to please his sinful nature, from that nature will reap destruction; the one who sows to please the Spirit, from the Spirit will reap eternal life." Although the original word in the Greek means "to sneer or to scorn," the English word "mock" is instructive when it comes to living together. "To mock" means "to imitate, to pretend in order to deceive." You can't do that to God without consequences, and you can't do that with marriage. Living together is literally a mockery or imitation of marriage in that it does not require a public commitment or lifetime vow of faithfulness.

o **1 Thessalonians 4:3-6** – "It is God's will that you should ... avoid sexual immorality; that each of you should learn to control his own body in a way that is holy and honorable, not in passionate lust like the heathen, who do not know God; and that in this matter no one should wrong his brother or take advantage of him." To "wrong" someone in this verse means "to exceed the proper limits." To "take advantage" means "to defraud, or to take more than you're entitled to." It is the picture of someone who takes more than they should while selfishly disregarding the best interests of others. When we live together, we exceed the limits God has set for us. We take more than we're entitled to.

o **Hebrews 13:4** – "Marriage should be honored by all, and the marriage bed kept pure, for God will judge the adulterer and all the sexually immoral." The marriage bed can only be kept pure when the sexual relationship is kept within marriage. Anything else brings God's judgment. Do you love your partner? Then why would you invite God's judgment into their life? Why would you willfully rob them of God's blessing?

(The above commentary and scriptures taken from www.rayfowler.org).

- **What about oral sex since we're not penetrating?**
  - o I submit that any type of touching or foreplay is in sin. God doesn't mean for our bodies to be in affection manners until marriage. We must refrain our sexual appetite (which is normal) until the confines and blessing of marriage before a holy God.

- **What about masturbation? As long as I'm not sleeping around, what's wrong with it?**
  - o There are several reasons why masturbation is not holy.
  - o First of all, when you masturbate you keep your sexual appetite alive. We need to kill our flesh (in the spirit) daily and keep that appetite suppressed until the right timing of God.
  - o Secondly, when you masturbate, you must consider that when you marry and you have already experienced your ecstasy because you know what your body likes and your new spouse cannot fulfill that for you somehow, you may resort back to just pleasing yourself versus trying to work it out with your spouse and working to fulfill the ecstasy together. This is just one situation to consider.

o Another situation to consider is once you open that door, your appetite for pleasure may increase and the devil may tempt you to fulfill that need through other means (toys or people). It is better to just shut the gate!

As a single person, it is much better when we can give all of our affections to our true husband, which is Jesus Christ. When our affections are not split between him and another lover, it is to our advantage. We can walk in unbridled love and affection towards the one who wants us to be the best person we can be! We can become the person that our future spouse will need and want. We can use the time of preparation for that marriage to our advantage and please our heavenly father at the same time!

Homosexuality and Transgenderism

Both of these represent an identity crisis within an individual. Both of these are unnatural in all its ways and not acceptable to God. First I will address transgender tendencies.

- An evident identity crisis and accepting in your heart the belief that a person is not the sex that God designed for them based upon their private parts, means that the person is demonically influenced. How do I say that? I say it because the person has agreed with the demons that are speaking into their ears with lies with such things as, "You are not a male. You are really a female. Look how you like dolls. See how you do this and that." Whenever the human agrees with the lies, it opens the door for the demon to enter and take over. This is why this book is written so that we may expose the enemy and his plan.

- We will tell the truth and allow God to fertilize the seed being planted.
  - When God created you, He knew exactly what He was doing. Sometimes our behaviors are based upon environmental influences. This has been proven scientifically as well through some studies. Demons can influence children as well. As parents, we are responsible to God on how we raise our children to cultivate their identity in Christ and to strengthen who they are as males and females.
  - I strongly encourage counseling and deliverance so that you can break all ties and unions you made with the enemy and become free. Shut that gate!

Virginity as a Christian

We must address virginity and chastity within the Bride of Christ. Although it looks like there's not any virgins left in the world, there most certainly is a huge amount of people who are preserving their bodies for the one that God has for them.

It is not easy to maintain your virginity, but it is possible. With God's help all things are possible. The Lord desires for us to preserve our bodies for the one person He has for us. Yes, the devil tries to remove the light from within you, but God will help you to overcome and be victorious in this area. In other areas of this book we talk about the many ways you can preserve your temple and remain pure before the Lord. Even if you have messed up in the past…God can restore you to virginity in the spirit and make all things new. He may not restore the Hyman, but can in spirit.

A Virgin Experience from a 30-year-old virgin male

There seems to be nothing more elusive than the ever-cherished or in some cases not-so-cherished virginity in our modern culture. It almost seems that our young people put their virginity on the auction block and wait for the highest bid. I must admit that I have been tempted many times to give up this wonderful gift that belongs to God and my future wife.

I can remember struggling in many instances in my life because the temptation was so immense. I now realize that God had his hand on my life even during the time I was backslidden from him. There were times that I would wonder why all of my peers, even at church, were having sex sometimes three and four times a week.

They seem to be the first ones to marry, have children, and gain wealth. The odd thing was that the same people who I went to church with would also go to school and youth events to have wild crazy sex while still finding time to make fun of me and look like little Christmas angels to the youth leadership.

I even found myself wishing to have sex so that I could beat these kids at their own game. What I did not realize is that if I would have had sex it would have caused trouble for me spiritually. Now you see why it was so easy for me to backslide. I am still amazed that God protected my virginity while I was backslidden from him. I couldn't believe it once I realized it! The reason is because when I was backslidden I hung with a group of people who were heavily involved in all manner of sexual activity.

At one point I was even asked if I wanted to be involved, but my girlfriend's mother stepped in and said not until I turned 18 because she wanted my girlfriend and I to wait until we were 18. I thank God every day for protecting me and keeping me pure in His service.

After coming through a period of backsliding I find that it made it more joyous than I could imagine. I found that I was more determined than ever to wait because the Father in Heaven brought me back to a relationship with him.

I am also very happy because the person I am going to marry has waited as well. I never thought He would give me someone who is so incredibly more beautiful than I could ever possibly dream of.

It seems that through this time of waiting I have learned so much about how much God loves us and how special it really is that God would send His only son to die for our sins. I know the beauty of my redeemer because I have waited for the woman I am going to marry.

I must say that I am so incredibly overjoyed at all that the Father in Heaven had done for me since I have decided to give everything I am to Him and Him alone. He has been so wonderful to me in ways that I cannot even describe. I cannot even describe my expectations of my upcoming wedding to the woman God gave me. This will be the prize worth waiting for. I will know that God has a beautiful experience waiting on the other side of the wedding nuptials. It will be worth it all!

Above Written By: Jimmy from Texas

It is not easy remaining a virgin until you marry, but God will surely bless you when it happens. Hang on Bride!

---

1 Corinthians 6:13 -2 0 13 Meats for the belly, and the belly for meats: but God shall destroy both it and them. Now the body is not for fornication, but for the Lord; and the Lord for the body.

14 And God hath both raised up the Lord, and will also raise up us by his own power.

15 Know ye not that your bodies are the members of Christ? shall I then take the members of Christ,

and make them the members of an harlot? God forbid.

16 What? know ye not that he which is joined to an harlot is one body? for two, saith he, shall be one flesh.

17 But he that is joined unto the Lord is one spirit.

18 Flee fornication. Every sin that a man doeth is without the body; but he that committeth fornication sinneth against his own body.

19 What? know ye not that your body is the temple of the Holy Ghost which is in you, which ye have of God, and ye are not your own?

20 For ye are bought with a price: therefore glorify God in your body, and in your spirit, which are God's.

As far as homosexuality, this is another beast. The Spirit of Antichrist is really pushing homosexuality so that it can taint the Bride. It is unhealthy in all its ways because it is so unnatural.

- **What's the big deal with homosexuality? Who are you to tell me who I can love? I can't change my heart. I follow it and it tells me who to love. The world accepts it, why can't the church?**

  - Homosexuality is wrong because God says it is. The church didn't make the rules, God did. We just follow the word of God and its precepts. I'll show scriptures in next question.

  - As far as not telling you who to love; please remember that the heart is deceitful (according to the Bible). We can't trust the heart or our feelings. We must trust the word of God over how we may feel about it in the natural or in the flesh. God is not flesh. He is spirit. He is holy and no sin shall stand in His presence.

  - As far as the argument of love goes, this is what I say to people. "What if I wanted to love a married man? My feelings tell me he is sexy and I want him and I don't care if he's married. I want…I want." You would say, "No…he is married…that's adultery and wrong." Or you may say, "So what? They are two consenting adults and they can have sex if they want to. It doesn't matter about the wife." Or you may say, "You must follow your heart and do it."

o I also say, "Well what if I want to love my 10 year-old nephew, or my 90 year-old father, or my 25 year-old daughter and we want to have sex and get married?"

o You may say, "No, that's incest and wrong. You can't do that." My reply, "So now we have a moral standard." Then if that still doesn't get to their heart, then I say, "OK, what if I want to marry my dog? Have sex with my dog? I love him. He's loyal. We have a special relationship and I'm in love." The point is; where do we draw the line? We draw the line at the word of God. So shut the gate!

- **Why is it unnatural? What does the Bible say about it?**

  o It is unnatural because God the Creator didn't design your body to work that way. We know that the man enters a penis into the anus of another man. This is unnatural as this brings diseases. The women bring in objects to penetrate the woman since they cannot satisfy the woman otherwise. It is unnatural because God meant sex to be between man and woman in the confines of marriage.

  o I also hear you say, "Well, what if they don't have sex?" My answer is the heart. You can be a homosexual by heart but not be having sex. When you AGREE WITH THE ENEMY THAT YOU ARE HOMOSEXUAL, then you are allowing the demon to enter and overtake your lustful passions.

- o When you battle with this demon all the time and you're trying not to give in to the temptations when you feel everything in you is pulling you to be homosexual, it is a demon controlling you.
- o I encourage you to get counseling and deliverance. It is neither natural nor healthy to be homosexual. It is a demonically-led lifestyle.

Here are scriptures about homosexuality:

Leviticus 18:22 "Do not practice homosexuality, having sex with another man as with a woman. It is a detestable sin.

Leviticus 20:13 "If a man practices homosexuality, having sex with another man as with a woman, both men have committed a detestable act. They must both be put to death, for they are guilty of a capital offense.

1 Corinthians 6:9 Don't you realize that those who do wrong will not inherit the Kingdom of God? Don't fool yourselves. Those who indulge in sexual sin, or who worship idols, or commit adultery, or are male prostitutes, or practice homosexuality,

1 Timothy 1:10 The law is for people who are sexually immoral, or who practice homosexuality, or are slave traders, liars, promise breakers, or who do anything else that contradicts the wholesome teaching

- **How is the Bible still relevant today when the whole world is accepting this practice?**
    - o The Bible is always relevant no matter what current culture is doing.
    - o We always live by the word of God. God changes not.
    - o Although the world is accepting of this behavior, the Bible is not and thus God is not. The Bible says that we are not of this world. (Jn. 17:16).
    - o Thus, we cannot participate in this wickedness. We must separate ourselves from this sin.

- **How can you say that demons are a part of this? This is not a choice, it is my heart and I'm born this way.**
    - o Demons are as real as you reading this book. The Bible says that our battle is not with flesh and blood, but with the principalities and powers of the air. (Eph. 6:12). Demons live to influence us and try to encourage us to believe their lies. When we agree with their lies, then it gives them rights to come in and opens a huge gate. Shut that gate!
    - o You are not born that way. God does not go against his own word. We must renew our minds with the word of God. Reading the Bible and confessing with our mouths that God is the healer, etc.
    - o Going through healing and deliverance is a great benefit to the Body of Christ to shut the doors and gates that were opened in our past.

- **What does purity have to do with my decision to love the same sex? At least we're humans.**
  - Yes, you are human, but it's no different than bestiality. It's all sodomy. Sodomy is unnatural in all its ways.
  - We must choose to put flesh under the will and subjection to God's word.
  - Shut the gate to perversion.

Sex with Demons or Spiritual World

This issue must be addressed because this is a growing trend with staggering numbers. Whenever God tells me to write a book, He will put situations in my life for me to write about and share with the Bride. When I had people contact me who was having sex with demons and really believing that it's ecstasy prayers with Jesus; I knew I had to include this in the book. Through my research and hearing the confessions of some people I interviewed, they trace it back to a term called "Bridal Paradigm."

This doctrine teaches that we must look at things through the lens of being the personal Bride of Christ. Although I agree with the main thought to this, some of the terminology used in this doctrine and music has been accused of causing others to go to the next level of having sex with this demon (or they think is Jesus).

The demon is actually called Incubus or Succubus. They are male and female demons that have sex with humans.

There is so much research you could find about those two, so I'm just merely leading you in the right direction.

I have actually experienced this before. One night during my sleep, I had the sheets roll back on my bed. I thought it was so real and I had a man in the bed with me. He spread my legs and went downtown – (slang for oral sex). He then began to make love to me and it was so passionate and soft. It felt so real. I finally caught on to this not being a dream but real and I woke up commanding that thing to leave my room! The next morning I confronted my son and said, "Someone in the house has opened the door to the enemy because a demon tried to have sex with me last night." He replied, "You too? It did me too! I believe it was that guy we moved in here that is homeless. I caught him on porno on the computer last night." So, needless to say we made him leave. The point is that the demon was so real and felt so authentic. I can see why people can be deceived and think this thing is real.

One of the ladies that contacted me about my ministry, We are the Bride Ministries, and was so excited thinking I had the revelation that she does about Jesus being my husband. She began to explain how she has built a relationship with this entity that she calls Jesus. I tried to explain that it's a demon. I asked her, "Why would Jesus need to enter that hole when He's already inside you?" I tried to reason with her but it didn't work.

Let me tell you how hers began. She said that she was at church late one night making a bulletin board and she was leaving the church when this voice spoke to her.

It convinced her to go back in the building that he wanted to marry her. She goes back in the building and she has this supernatural experience where she believes she's really marrying the Lord.

Then, he slams her on the floor and makes love to her in the sanctuary and has been ever since. So, she believes it is Jesus. This thing makes love to her all the time and she loves it. She said he is so gentle with her and tells her how much he loves her. It's an imposter!

I then met this other lady who told me I'm going to make a whole lot of people mad in high places if I write against this book.

She told me that it's bigger than I think and in her experience, she meets this married man in a building every day in intercessory prayer and they both have sex with Jesus together. He undresses her and helps her to have sex with Jesus. She told me that she knows of couples who make bedrooms dedicated to intimacy with Jesus and they go in there specifically to have sex with this entity together as a couple. So, let's talk about this:

- **I'm not having sex with demons; I'm having sex with Jesus. It is passion and bridal love for my creator. How can this be demonic when it feels so real and is so passionate and erotic?**
  - If you cannot do it in public at the alter in front of the church and in the wide open, it's not of God! Why would God want you to hide and be secretive about his intimacy with you? Yes, He wants you to pray in the privacy of the closet, but it can be done anywhere.
  - Demons can make it feel so erotic and passionate. They are very real.

- **The deception or misunderstanding of bridal intercession and bridal paradigm teaching and intimacy with God.**

  o I researched this doctrine. I can't find anything that is encouraging others to have sex with God or that intimacy includes sexual things.

  o Thus my conclusion is that people are taking this in the wrong manner.

  o Yes, Jesus is our husband and we will meet Him soon at the marriage supper of the lamb.

  o Yes, I agree with the teaching about the fire of God, the passionate lover that He is, etc. So, I cannot conclude that this doctrine is encouraging people to get under the sheets go into this sexual encounter with demons.

  o One person suggested for me to read the book forwarded by Mike Bickle called *Bridal Intercession* by Gary Weins. I read the book and still cannot see how the people that contacted me can justify what they are doing by this book. So, my conclusion is that these people are misinterpreting the message from bridal intercession doctrine. If I am wrong, please inform me.

- **The Demons of Incubus and Succubus.**

  o These demons are very real. I encourage you to research them if you question what I am saying.

  o This lady speaks out about these demons, "A former stripper turned ministry leader who claims she once considered becoming a lesbian has offered up a rather unusual explanation for homosexuality. In an article for Charisma magazine, writer Cedric Harmon interviews a woman named Contessa Adams who claims that she was once possessed by sexual demons. Adams claims repeated attacks by a succubus — defined in the article as a female sexual demon that traditionally assaults men — made her contemplate becoming a lesbian." This article further explains, "These spiritual rapists, as Adams describes them in her book, *Consequences*, often prey on people by performing sexual acts through nightmares and erotic dreams. Some people become so dependent upon these demonic experiences that they actually look forward to them. "Anybody that has been attacked by them will tell you ... they're worried [that] they could not find that pleasure with mortal people," says Adams, who claims she was once possessed by sexual demons. The two most identifiable sexual demons are the incubus, which is a male sexual demon that traditionally assaults women, and the succubus, which is a female sexual demon that assaults men. Sometimes they also lure people into homosexual behaviors. Adams notes that one evangelist, whose name she would not divulge, was so troubled by the sexual pleasure the succubus gave her that she even contemplated suicide.

- o Adams says the succubus spirit that used to attack her confused her so much that she contemplated becoming a lesbian. "Unless you're strong enough to rebuke it, they'll keep coming back," she says. "You must speak the Word of God, knowing you have power in the name of Jesus." Eddie Smith, the president of U.S. Prayer Track and a respected leader in deliverance ministry, believes that experiences like Adams' are common. He and his wife, Alice, have ministered to "at least hundreds" of people suffering from demonic sexual attacks. "Many people don't realize that there is even historic documentation of this," Smith told Charisma.

- o He says that it is especially common in pagan religions such as Santeria and voodoo because people who practice those religions invoke demons to come and interact with them." (Harmon, 2012)

- **What's wrong with having a spiritual wife or husband and having sex with it? At least I'm not at risk for a sexually transmitted disease, etc.**

  - o I can hear some of you saying this. "What is wrong with this…at least I'm not having sex with a human." My answer is that it is unnatural. These demons are not good. They are doing it to rob you spiritually. Believe me, there is a whole lot more going on than just merely sex. Shut that gate!

o If you are having sex with demons, I encourage you to find someone who believes in casting demons out and seek counsel and deliverance from both you and the home where you are experiencing this demonic encounter.

o Another thing to consider is that God is spirit. Why would He need to satisfy your flesh? The life of Christianity is about dying to our flesh. God would not work the flesh. Shut the gate!

Sex with Animals – Bestiality

Another term for bestiality is zoophilia. This is the legal term in many countries. This is being practiced today and it is a huge growing trend. This practice involves a human having sexual acts with an animal. This is unnatural and unhealthy in all its ways as well. This is what the Bible says about bestiality:

The Bible mentions bestiality in four different passages. **Exodus 22:19** says, "Anyone who has sexual relations with an animal must be put to death." **Leviticus 18:23** declares, "Do not have sexual relations with an animal and defile yourself with it. A woman must not present herself to an animal to have sexual relations with it; that is a perversion." **Leviticus 20:15-16** commands, "If a man has sexual relations with an animal, he must be put to death, and you must kill the animal. If a woman approaches an animal to have sexual relations with it, kill both the woman and the animal. They must be put to death; their blood will be on their own heads." **Deuteronomy 27:21** agrees, "Cursed is the man who has sexual relations with any animal."

You may be surprised at how many countries where this is legal. According to Independent Magazine, "Sex acts with animals are legal in Canada, so long as there is no penetration involved, according to a surprise ruling issued by the Supreme Court." (Garcia, 2016). Many countries and in many places in the US make it legal now for bestiality/zoophilia.

Charisma Magazine has written many articles about this subject. "This leads us to *Broad City* going down a new avenue, bestiality." (Louder, 2016).

News Busters, which is an online liberal media watcher website, wrote, "The sophomore TV Land show *Younger,* about a 40-year-old divorcée who pretends to be 26 to get a job in the New York publishing industry, shocked viewers with a scene of bestiality this week." (Coombs, 2016).

The list could go on and on; however, I submit to you that once the world opened the door to open homosexuality acceptance, that it then opened the door to bestiality.

I believe this is the beginning of what we will see. Shut the gates.

Perversions, Addictions & Fetishes

There are many people out there that have obsessions with many things such as feet, hands, toys, etc. Too much of anything is probably led by a demon. God does not want us addicted to things or behaviors because they then become idols to us. The Lord revealed to me one time that when a person leans on something when they are hurting (drinking, smoking, sex, drugs, etc); that it is an idol. We put that obsession or need above God. Ask God to take that desire from you. He may lead you to go see your pastor, go through deliverance, or to repent and renounce something. The Holy Spirit is our guide.

Purity in the Bedroom Spiritually

Not only does the Lord want you to have purity in sex in the bedroom, but in prayer as well. I presented the case that sex between husband and wife may be spiritual warfare. I saw a movie one time where it showed the angels outside the house of a married couple and this demon walked up to the window and wanted to "peep in" on this Christian couple having sex. The angel threw his sword out and kicked that demon off the property and told him that was a holy moment and he's not allowed to watch. I think about how God created that to be as such.

So, in prayer we get on our knees and fight in spiritual warfare in the bedroom. The bedroom should be as much a holy place as the sanctuary at church because we encounter God in prayer as well as the holy union of husband and wife. It is not an act to be ashamed and feel like you're hiding it from God. He created it now enjoy it.

5

EXAMPLES OF SEX AND DESTINY CONSEQUENCES

The Lord gave me a dream right before I finished the book and told me to include stories of sex and how it affected destinies. Sex can cut off a destiny so quick. The following are real life stories. I will not list names to respect identities.

25 Years of Setback

Using my life as an example, my books explain how the perverted expression of sex and addiction caused me to miss out on over 20 years of ministry. If I was healed and whole back when my ministry first started when I was 20 years old, then where would I be today? I surely would not be here coming out of the pit and starting from the bottom. On the other side, if it was not for my testimony, these books would not have been birthed. I don't live in regret; I press forward to where my hope comes from! I merely wanted to point out that it has definitely hindered me from my maximum potential in the kingdom. On the other hand, God has promised to restore me and it will be double reward for my submission to His will!

Seducing Devil to Steal a Ministry

I think of a woman minister who is a praise and worship leader and very anointed! She was rising in God in ministry. She was hosting conferences, traveling all over the United States ministering and she had a following on Facebook of about 6,000 people who were out of church because they felt cast out.

These people were prophetic and the churches had dismissed their gifts, etc. So, this woman I'm speaking about caught on to the fact that these people could have an "online church." So, it was growing huge. There was another minister who had the same type of vision and he had thousands of followers. They merged together the visions but made a mistake at one of the conferences and slept together. The enemy came in through lust. He is married and she is single. It ended up being exposed and he denied it to everyone but totally trashed her on Facebook. He defamed her character and attempted to turn her followers against her and to follow him. Prior to this, he tried very hard to have her hand over her ministry to him. It somehow got exposed when she refused to hand it over. So, he basically ruined her and stayed married. Six months later he is still running his empire and she is in a deep, dark pit.

She called me one day and said, "June, I really admire you being a single woman and holding your purity. PLEASE DON'T DO WHAT I DID AND LOSE IT IN ONE NIGHT! She began to explain that she was like me and held her purity and consecration for years but this man seduced her on the phone long before he met her in person. He then made his move and destroyed her. He is still ministering.

So, one year goes by and she's trying to make a comeback but it's like she's been set back 100 years. She is having to start all over.

One night of pleasure. One moment of weakness. One sin. Cost her everything.

Loneliness and Codependency Is a Killer

There are so many stories I could write about but loneliness is one way the enemy works against people. He can even work against a married person that is lonely. They may leave their spouse to find someone else who will fill that void. Our void must be found in Jesus.

Also remember that loneliness is a feeling. We can't rely on feelings. We must rely on the word of God and His truth. His truth says we are fulfilled in Him. We do not need other people to fulfill our lives.

Now, I'm not a counselor, but I do have experience with codependency. This is the same as loneliness because you feel like you have to have someone there with you. We can also create idols out of people. Remember, anything we put before God is an idol and He may require it of you.

The Consequences of Sexual Sin

We all know of the consequences of sickness and sexual sin. Sexually transmitted diseases were basically born out of pre-marital sex. Some STD's will kill you or have no cure.

Even if we do not obtain an STD, we still have consequences such as soul-ties. I'm far from the expert on soul-ties but I will tell you that it is a very serious exchange that happens when you have sex with someone.

You are literally giving a part of you away that can only be returned to you through repentance and healing/deliverance. When you have sex with someone outside the bounds of marriage, you gain a soul-tie with that person.

This means that who they slept with prior and the souls of those people are all mixed in with one person. So, if you sleep with Johnny Joe and he has slept with 100 people, you will then receive from all of those! Until you go through deliverance and healing/repentance, that soul-tie is still with you. If you do not believe me please go to see the expert, Dr. Phillip Morris at www.drphillipmorris.com. He will help you to find your deliverance.

Another consequence is depression and oppression. Some people go through emotional disorders when they feel the shame and guilt following the act. The devil will wear a Christian out because they fell. This can cause all types of other issues.

Another consequence is pride. A person may bury the sin within their heart and justify their actions and this furthers their relationship from God. They begin to not pray anymore because they do not want to face what they have done. They will just harden their heart.

Another consequence is the penalty that sin may bring from God. For instance, David and Bathsheba in the Bible. He lusted after a woman on the top of a roof while she was bathing. He wanted her so band and got her pregnant while husband was at war. They covered it up by killing the husband. Although he ended up being exposed to the prophet and heard the consequence of his first-born son dying, he did repent to God. His son still died and David paid a great price for that sexual sin.

There are so many other stories in the Bible about people who had sex in the wrong way and had to pay a great price. Their price might not be paid immediately, but it will come.

Dr. June Dawn Knight

6
HOW TO SHUT THE GATES

The Lord desires for us to live a holy and pure life so that we can be all that He has called us to be. He wants us walking a life of fasting, prayer, and consecration to do His will and purposes on the Earth. We only have one life to live and we need not waste it on trying to fulfill the lusts of our flesh. We are not meant to live to satisfy our earthly and fleshly desires. We are meant to live the fullness of the destiny that God means for us to complete.

I talk about this in my book, *Organic Christianity; Back to the Garden*. God wrote each human's book before time began and I can just hear Him saying, "Here's what we want June to do for us when she surrenders all. We want her to reveal to mankind this aspect of who we are." Their will (God the Father, God the Son and God the Holy Ghost – The Trinity – The three-in-one godhead), is so much better than our will. Their desire is for each human to reveal to mankind another aspect of who they are. They want us to be unique and allow God to use us to the fullest capacity possible.

It is so sad when people die and never complete their destiny. They only had one life to live and they wasted it on trying to fulfill a lustful desire or natural life. They never walked in the supernatural or discovered the supernatural. What a sad life.

Well you that are reading this book have a chance to not live a sad life. You can live a fulfilled life by shutting all the gates to the enemy of your body. Tell him NO and shut that gate.

How do you shut the gates?

We shut the gates by doing an about-face and turning from our wicked ways. Get on our face before God and repent for all of our sins of the past. Get counseling and allow God to cleanse our innermost being from all doors and gates that we opened from our past. Deal with our issues and break all curses, agreements, words, etc., that brought the actions of sin in our lives.

Going through deliverance is not a bad thing. It's a good thing because we break every tie to the enemy in our lives. We examine our hearts before God and allow Him to cleanse those dark spots and wrinkles. Be clean today!

Things to Consider Before Dating Someone

When I talk to people about dating, I share a revelation the Lord gave me about how God desires for a couple to come together in marriage and here it is:

When a person is single, they should write out what they desire in a mate and be specific. God wants to know what your heart's desire is for a mate. Here are a few of mine (to give you an example):

- Must love Jesus more than me
- Must be spirit-filled and speak in tongues
- Must know how to go to war in the prayer closet with me
- Loves to worship

- Funny sense of humor
- Gentle and a great listener
- Allows me to remain unique and child-like in my faith
- Loves romance & intimacy, Etc.

So, God takes that list and now Jo-Blow wants to consider marrying me. They must go to the father and say, "Lord, I want to date June with the consideration to marry her. What do you say?" Then God replies, "Okay, if you want to marry her, then you need to change. I know what she wants so just start trusting me every day and I'll lead you down the right path." God wants to prepare both you and the future spouse. This is why time is of the essence. Now, if you've known each other for a long time, you've probably already gained the traits required, etc., but the point is to seek God for that future mate.

Then, when you date there are boundaries. You date only with the intention to consider marrying that person. Why waste a person's time? It will only arouse the flesh, so we do not open that door. When we date a prospective spouse, we respect them as their position in the Lord that this is God's child first. NOT MINE. Even when we get married they are still not MINE. They are God's child. We must always keep that position in mind because it will allow us to keep that child before His father who knows them very well. We lean on God and not that person. This is key in the relationship. They are only human. This is why we have this great relationship with God before you begin the mate process.

So, while you're dating you keep boundaries like do not be alone in risky situations that may cause your flesh to rile up.
We do not go to bars or drink strong drink that would cause us

to lose our defenses. We try to keep everything in the relationship open so that your good may not be evil spoken of.

We do not talk about sex unless it pre-marriage and in that case it should be talked about so that you both have an understanding before the honeymoon. This of course is within the bounds of keeping fleshly lusts out that would cause you to act on it prior to marriage. The Bible says if you cannot refrain then go ahead and marry to prevent you from burning in Hell. This is how serious fornication is.

When you are considering a mate, make sure it is someone of your equal faith. Unequally yoked is more than just Christian and non-Christian. It is faith and mission. You want to date someone that you are marching beside and not dragging to the alter. You cannot date someone who is carnal-minded. When you marry your heart and vision is going one way and he may have no vision. It's an unequal situation. You may be kingdom-minded and he may be wanting to watch TV all the time, or her. So, make sure you are in unison on mission and goals for the new family.

Discuss child-bearing issues such as discipline, going to church, family extensions such as your parents and their parents, etc. How does your future spouse feel about children, etc.?

Build your prayer life from the beginning. Before I even consider a man I will say, "Let me hear you pray." This is a priority to me because if we can't war together in the spirit, then I'm wasting my time because my life is a spiritual warfare. I live in constant warfare because of my ministry, the media, etc. If I don't have someone that I know can cover my back in prayer, then I'm wasting my time. So, pray with them and get to know how they interact with God. How do they respond to the enemy? In other words, what kind of soldier are they in the Army of the Living God?

Take time to learn how they interact on a daily basis with God. How do they handle pressure? Do they fall on their face in prayer and seek God first or do they get angry, etc? Do they call momma and listen to her advice more than they listen to God? Who are they codependent upon?

When the pressure is on, that is how you will learn a person. What is their character and integrity when the heat is turned up? How can you know unless you spend time with that person?

As a minister, I believe that men should minister to men and women to women. This is to protect both sides. If you are both ministers, then you should keep this standard. You can begin to learn boundaries between each other in both ministry and in every day life.

So, when you consider dating someone, then you must:
- Are they a Christian?
- Are they same faith as me?
- Are they as spiritual or have it close to my understanding of God?
- Do our missions go hand-in-hand? Our outlook on future?
- Does that person respect my body enough to not touch it until the day that God is honored in our temples?
- Has that person been delivered of previous soul-ties?

(This is a requirement as you should be delivered as well).

- Is that person healed of all past relationships without getting angry when you talk about one of their previous ones?
- Are they 100% whole to where they're not living in the past?
- Do they know how to pray and how to rely upon God and not me as their spouse?
- How do my friends and family feel about this partnership? Are there any red flags within my circle of influence? If so...I need to step back and pray and seek God before proceeding further.
- Do I see my relationship with God advancing forward in a greater way being with this person or does it seem to be going backward with God? (This is a huge tell-tale sign).
- Do I feel peace about spending the rest of my life with this person?

Last Words From Author

I pray this book has blessed you and encouraged you to examine your hearts about your views towards sex and your body. Please, I'm not asking you to take my words for gospel. I'm merely asking you to go before God in prayer and ask Him if what I'm revealing to you is truth and let Him resonate it in your heart.

I have been divorced so I understand being in messed-up relationships based upon our history.

I just encourage you to read the book, "Love and Respect by Eggerichs" and it will help you a lot. After reading his book I greatly repented and saw many mistakes I made in the past. God is revealing this to me now so that I can have a healthy future and give God all the glory for the healing He has done in my life.

God bless you Bride.

7
PRAYER FOR DELIVERANCE AND FREEDOM

The Lord wants us free from any demonic oppression or possession. God wants us walking in freedom, purity, consecration and in the beauty of His holiness. Let's come together in agreement today so that you can be fulfilled and be all that He wrote about in your Book of Destiny.

Lord, I come before you today and I surrender all of myself to your will. I ask you Lord to reveal my heart to me. Your word says that you are the searcher of man's hearts and I'm asking you to expose the enemy's lies in my life and bring those things to the surface so that I may deal with them and be set free.

I ask you Lord to forgive me for giving my body over to any other person except the spouse that you meant for me. Forgive me Lord for having other lovers before you. Cleanse my body and my soul before you today Lord. I plead the blood of Jesus over my temple today and ask you to cleanse it by the washing of your word.

Lord, please use me for your glory according to the book that you wrote about me before time began in my Book of Destiny.

Help me Lord to fulfill my destiny for you. Help me to live a fasted lifestyle and to learn to keep my body under subjection to your will and purposes. I speak to you body and I tell you that you will listen to the will of the Lord and bow down to His will first in my life. I command you to obey God.

I love you Lord and I thank you for saving my soul and taking me to my destiny. In Jesus' name! Amen!

ABOUT THE AUTHOR

Dr. June Knight is a specialist on corporate communications, social media, corporations (ministry) media, and communication implementation. Dr. June has served ministries and businesses all over the world to achieve their goals. She partners with leaders and God to obtain the ideal outcome for the vision God placed on the inside of them. Whether it is communicating to a community, a congregation, a nation, or a certain targeted niche, Dr. June helps the visionary to articulate the vision and implement a strategy to obtain maximum effectiveness.

Dr. June's Education:

• Bachelor's Degree in Public Relations at Austin Peay State University
• Master's Degree in Corporate Communications at APSU
• One year of studies at World Harvest Bible College
• Doctorate of Theology at International Miracle Institute

While in Graduate School at APSU, Dr. June studied in London (Winter 2011/2012) and studied under the top three global marketing/advertising/communication firms in the world. She wrote a 20-page research paper comparing how the United Kingdom markets a product versus the United States. Dr. June completed the class with a grade of 100! Following graduation, Dr. June turned that paper into her first book, Mark of the Beast.

Dr. June has written five books and owns a publishing company

– <u>TreeHouse Publishers</u>. She also is the President and CEO of <u>We are the Bride Ministries</u> which includes: <u>WATB.tv</u>, <u>WATB Radio</u>, & <u>WATB Center</u>. She is a TV and Radio Host and is hosting two television shows: <u>TOSS – The Original State Show</u> and <u>BRIDE TIME LIVE</u>.

Dr. June's heart is UNITY in the Bride of Christ. Her goal is to close the gap on communications within the Bride through radio, television, social media and publishing. She understands the importance of communicating your vision so that others may understand and engage. Her greatest gift is critiquing businesses and ministries on how they are communicating the vision that God has given them. Dr. June then provides strategies and input into how they may be successful with their mission on Earth.

For more information on Dr. June go to:
www.drjune.org
www.wearethebride.us
www.watbradio.com
www.watb.tv
www.watbcenter.com
www.gotreehouse.org

Made in the USA
Middletown, DE
08 June 2020

96509518R00056